by
Charis Mather

Minneapolis, Minnesota

Credits:
All images are courtesy of Shutterstock.com, unless otherwise specified. With thanks to Getty Images, Thinkstock Photo, and iStockphoto. Front Cover – Paper Street Design, ONYXprj, Amanda Cardent, marotaroi. Images used on every page – Paper Street Design. 2–3 – marotaro. 4–5 – Frings Clement, LuckyStep, Viktoriya. 6–7 – Colin D. Young, joshimerbin, Olga Kulakova, Tragoolchitr Jittasaiyapan. 8–9 – alionapro, LingHK, Mopic, Pablo Carlos Budassi, CC BY-SA 4.0 <https-//creativecommons.org/licenses/by-sa/4.0>, via Wikimedia Commons, yurchak. 10–11 – Allexxandar, Elena Schweitzer, Lukasz Pawel Szczepanski, Milos Muller, VikiVector. 12–13 – Andreas Cellarius, Public domain, via Wikimedia Commons, Cristiano Banti, Public domain, via Wikimedia Commons, Gerrit Dou, No restrictions, via Wikimedia Commons, Joseph-Nicolas Robert-Fleury, Public domain, via Wikimedia Commons. 14–15 – Brian Donovan, Grygorieva, Iron Mary, Miceking, N.Vector Design, Valentina Kalashnikova. 16–17 – anatoliy_gleb, Antares_StarExplorer, fboudrias, Johannes Hevelius (28 January 1611 – 28 January 1687) Scanned by Torsten Bronger, 4 April 2003, Public domain, via Wikimedia CommonsOrion_constellation_Hevelius, Sidney_Hall_-_Urania's_Mirror_-_Canis_Major,_Lepus,_Columba_Noachi_&_Cela_Sculptoris. 18–19 – NASA, H. Ford (JHU), G. Illingworth (UCSC/LO), M.Clampin (STScI), G. Hartig (STScI), the ACS Science Team, and ESA, Public domain, via Wikimedia Commons, Pablo Carlos Budassi, CC BY-SA 4.0 <https-//creativecommons.org/licenses/by-sa/4.0>, via Wikimedia Commons. 22–23 – ESO, CC BY 4.0 <https-//creativecommons.org/licenses/by/4.0>, via Wikimedia Commons, Pablo Carlos Budassi, CC BY-SA 4.0 <https-//creativecommons.org/licenses/by-sa/4.0>, via Wikimedia Commons, Veronika By. 24–25 – Bjoern Wylezich, DiamondGalaxy, Evgeniyqw, sciencepics 26–27 – Blue Planet Studio, muratart, Tosaka, CC BY-SA 3.0 <http-//creativecommons.org/licenses/by-sa/3.0/>, via Wikimedia Commons. 28–29 – Aicrovision, hrui, Infrared: IPAC/NASA Ultraviolet: STScI (NASA), Public domain, via Wikimedia Commons. 30–32 – marotaro, Ground Picture, James Webb Space Telescope, CC BY 2.0 <https-//creativecommons.org/licenses/by/2.0>, via Wikimedia Commons.

Bearport Publishing Company Product Development Team
President: Jen Jenson; Director of Product Development: Spencer Brinker; Managing Editor: Allison Juda; Associate Editor: Naomi Reich; Associate Editor: Tiana Tran; Senior Designer: Colin O'Dea; Associate Designer: Elena Klinkner; Associate Designer: Kayla Eggert; Product Development Specialist: Anita Stasson

Library of Congress Cataloging-in-Publication Data is available at www.loc.gov or upon request from the publisher.

ISBN: 979-8-88509-947-9 (hardcover)
ISBN: 979-8-88822-120-4 (paperback)
ISBN: 979-8-88822-267-6 (ebook)

© 2024 BookLife Publishing
This edition is published by arrangement with BookLife Publishing.

North American adaptations © 2024 Bearport Publishing Company. All rights reserved. No part of this publication may be reproduced in whole or in part, stored in any retrieval system, or transmitted in any form or by any means, electronic, mechanical, photocopying, recording, or otherwise, without written permission from the publisher.

For more information, write to Bearport Publishing, 5357 Penn Avenue South, Minneapolis, MN 55419.

CONTENTS

For Your Eyes Only! 4
Star Basics 6
Types of Stars 8
Sun Secrets 10
Undercover Astronomers 12
Constellations 14
Star Stories 16
Hungry Galaxies 18
Vampire Stars 20
When Stars Die 22
Lucy the Diamond Star 24
Secret Star Sounds 26
Dyson Swarms 28
Your Mission 30

Glossary 31
Index 32
Read More 32
Learn More Online 32

FOR YOUR EYES ONLY!

The information you are about to read is top secret. Only special agents are allowed **access** to these files on some of the strangest things we know about stars. What are the dark secrets behind these bright objects in space?

There are some things in these files that leave even our top scientists scratching their heads. It's up to you to find out as much as you can about stars.

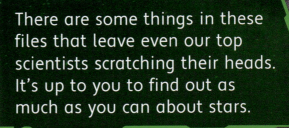

Please place your hand on the scanner to check your access level.... SCANNING...

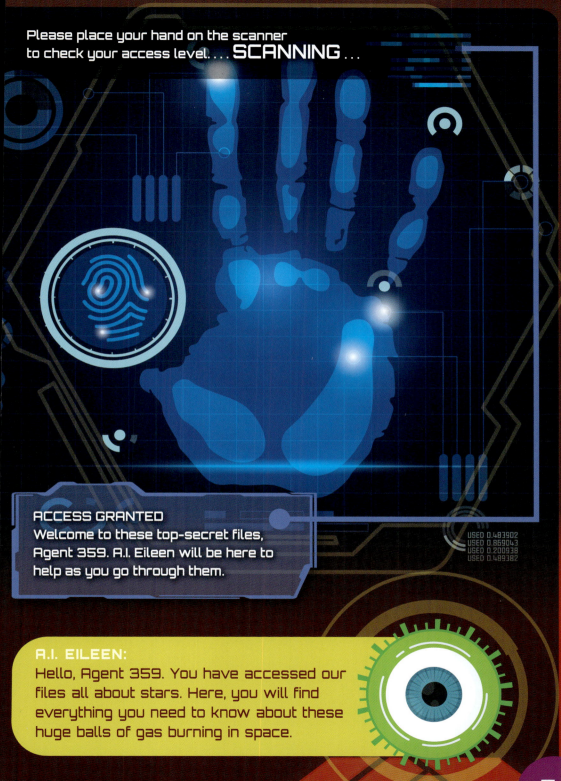

ACCESS GRANTED
Welcome to these top-secret files, Agent 359. A.I. Eileen will be here to help as you go through them.

USED 0.483902
USED 0.869043
USED 0.200938
USED 0.489382

A.I. EILEEN:
Hello, Agent 359. You have accessed our files all about stars. Here, you will find everything you need to know about these huge balls of gas burning in space.

STAR BASICS

A.I. EILEEN: To get you up to speed, here is some background information about stars.

It is possible to see thousands of stars from Earth. However, there are billions and billions of stars in the **universe**.

The light from distant stars has to travel very far to get to Earth. Scientists use the amount of time it takes for light to travel in a year, called a light-year, to measure the distance between space objects, including stars.

Even though they look small from Earth, stars are very big. The smallest stars that scientists know of are about 75,000 miles (120,000 km) across. That's so big that stars' **gravity** pulls in other objects. This makes planets and other space objects circle around stars.

A NORMAL STAR

PLANETS

Stars are made of burning gases. Their color is determined by how hot they burn. Hotter stars are blue or white. Cooler stars are red or brown. Yellow stars are in between in temperature.

HOTTER

COOLER

7

TYPES OF STARS

PROTOSTARS
Before a star forms, it is just a protostar. The protostar is made from gases in space. The force of gravity presses the gases into a cloud. Eventually, the gas cloud collapses, creating an explosion of heat and light. A star is born!

Protostars forming in a gas cloud

MAIN SEQUENCE STARS
As a protostar gets hotter and is squeezed more tightly together, it becomes a main sequence star. Most stars in the universe are main sequence stars.

A main sequence star is hotter than a protostar.

DWARF STARS

Many main sequence stars are dwarf stars. They are smaller and less bright than other kinds of stars.

A WHITE DWARF

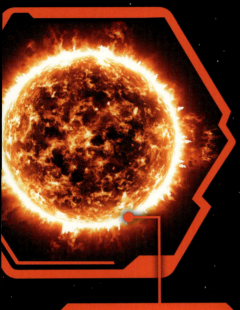

A RED GIANT STAR

GIANT AND SUPERGIANT STARS

The largest stars are giants and supergiants. Toward the ends of stars' lives, the **hydrogen** gases at their **cores** are turned into **helium**. This makes the stars blow up like balloons!

BETELGEUSE

ANTARES

GIANTS AND SUPERGIANTS

RIGEL

ALDEBARAN

9

SUN SECRETS

A.I. EILEEN: Earth travels around a star we call the sun.

TYPE: yellow dwarf, main sequence
SIZE ACROSS: about 865,000 miles (1.4 million km)
TEMPERATURE: 10,000 degrees Fahrenheit (5,500 degrees Celcius)
DISTANCE FROM EARTH: about 90 million miles (150 million km) away

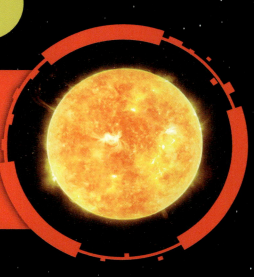

The sun does not look very big from Earth because it is far away. But actually, it is as big as 330,000 Earths put together.

The sun is at the center of our solar system. This includes a group of eight planets and other objects in space that move around, or **orbit**, the big star.

10

Without the sun, our planet would get very cold and dark. But it would be 8 minutes and 20 seconds before we would first feel the effects if the sun went out. That's how long it takes for the star's light to reach us.

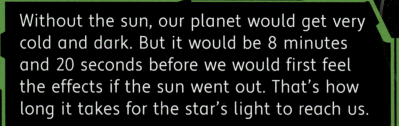

Without the sun's light and heat, most living things would die. The top layer of the oceans would turn to ice.

A.I. EILEEN: Don't worry! Scientists don't expect the sun to disappear anytime soon!

11

UNDERCOVER ASTRONOMERS

A.I. EILEEN:
Today, **astronomers** can share ideas about the sun and other stars freely. In the past, however, some powerful people thought Earth was at the center of the universe. These people were wrong, but they punished anyone who didn't agree with them.

A.I. EILEEN:
Unfortunately, this meant that some early astronomers had to hide what they learned. It took years for their work to eventually help future scientists understand space better.

NICOLAUS COPERNICUS

Nicolaus Copernicus figured out that Earth and the other planets in our solar system all circle around the sun. This could have gotten Copernicus in trouble. So, he kept his writings about it secret for many years.

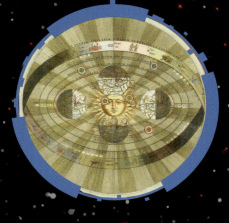

GALILEO GALILEI

Galileo Galilei was alive about 100 years after Copernicus. He used a **telescope** to find proof that Copernicus was right about the sun. However, when Galileo tried to share this knowledge, he was punished. He was never allowed to leave his house again.

GALILEO GETTING IN TROUBLE

13

CONSTELLATIONS

A.I. EILEEN:
Constellations are groups of stars in recognizable patterns or shapes. For years, people have used them to find their way around at night.

URSA MINOR

Some people say Ursa Minor looks like a bear. The constellation's name even means Little Bear. Ursa Minor contains the well-known North Star. People sometimes use this bright star to figure out what direction they are facing.

LITTLE BEAR

14

THE SOUTHERN CROSS

People in the Southern **Hemisphere** can use the Southern Cross to point themselves south. This constellation got its name because its stars are shaped like a cross. It's easy to see because the constellation's stars are much brighter than the other stars around it.

SOUTHERN CROSS

A.I. EILEEN: Several countries in the Southern Hemisphere have the Southern Cross on their flags.

FLAG OF AUSTRALIA

FLAG OF PAPUA NEW GUINEA

15

STAR STORIES

A.I. EILEEN: People have been telling stories about the **myths** and legends behind constellations for years.

ORION AND THE SCORPION
In Greek mythology, Orion was a great hunter who believed he could hunt every animal in the world. This made the gods angry at Orion. They sent a scorpion to stop him. After the scorpion defeated Orion, both hunter and scorpion were turned into constellations.

THE DOG STAR

Sirius, the brightest star in the night sky, is nicknamed The Dog Star. People in the past thought the star brought unusually warm days that would upset dogs and cause thunderstorms, floods, illnesses, and bad luck.

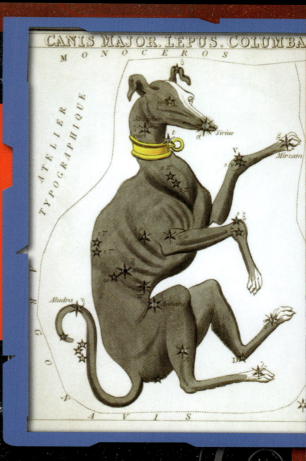

SIRIUS, THE DOG STAR

Does the Dog Star really cause hot weather? No. Even the brightest stars are too far away to affect Earth's temperature. For years, however, Sirius was often visible during the warmer months of the year.

HUNGRY GALAXIES

A.I. EILEEN:
Millions or billions of stars clump together with gas, dust, and other objects because of the pull of gravity. These groups are called galaxies. Sometimes, galaxies collide.

These two colliding galaxies are called the Mice Galaxies, named for the long taillike trails of stars and gas behind them.

When two differently sized galaxies smash together, the larger one may pull parts of the smaller galaxy into itself. The larger galaxy grows even bigger as it eats the smaller galaxy.

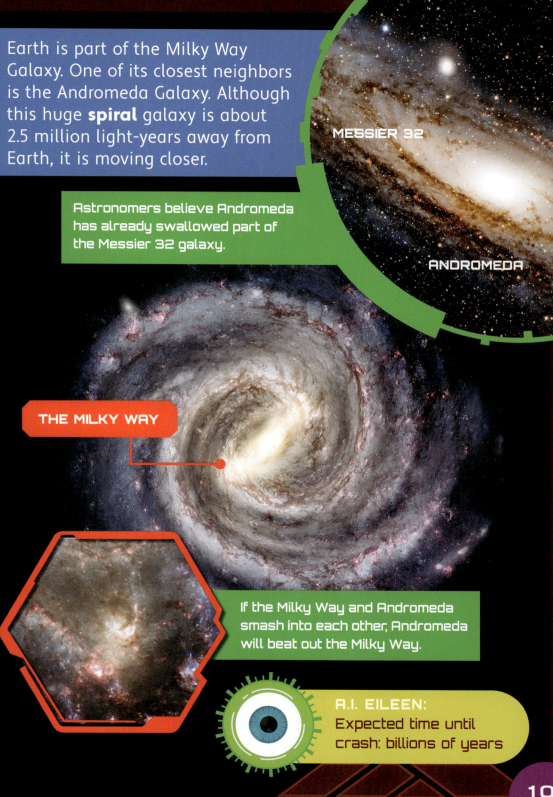

Earth is part of the Milky Way Galaxy. One of its closest neighbors is the Andromeda Galaxy. Although this huge **spiral** galaxy is about 2.5 million light-years away from Earth, it is moving closer.

MESSIER 32

Astronomers believe Andromeda has already swallowed part of the Messier 32 galaxy.

ANDROMEDA

THE MILKY WAY

If the Milky Way and Andromeda smash into each other, Andromeda will beat out the Milky Way.

A.I. EILEEN: Expected time until crash: billions of years

VAMPIRE STARS

Black holes are dark space objects that have superstrong gravity pulling things toward them. In 2020, scientists saw odd behavior between two stars in the HR 6819 group. Some thought it was evidence of a black hole. Others disagreed.

The gravity of a black hole sucks in everything nearby, even light. That's what makes them so dark.

Two teams joined up to share **equipment** in the hopes of finding out more about the stars in HR 6819. They decided there wasn't a black hole after all. Something else was going on.

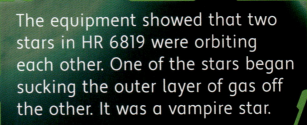

Scientists use very large telescopes like this.

The equipment showed that two stars in HR 6819 were orbiting each other. One of the stars began sucking the outer layer of gas off the other. It was a vampire star.

A.I. EILEEN:
Vampires myths tell stories about creatures that suck human blood. Unlike these creatures, vampire stars really exist.

21

WHEN STARS DIE

A.I. EILEEN: Stars go through different stages of death as they burn up all their **fuel**.

SMALL STAR DEATH

As a small- or medium-sized star uses up its fuel, it grows into a red giant. Eventually, its outer layers of gas and dust start to peel off. Once this is done, the star is a white dwarf. Eventually, it cools off and fades from view.

WHITE DWARF

BIG STAR DEATH

Once a big star's fuel is used up, the star collapses. The outer layers burst into a powerful and very bright explosion called a supernova. The collapsed center may become a black hole or a neutron star—a collapsed star core that gives off lots of energy and spins very fast.

SUPERNOVA
BLACK HOLE
NEUTRON STAR

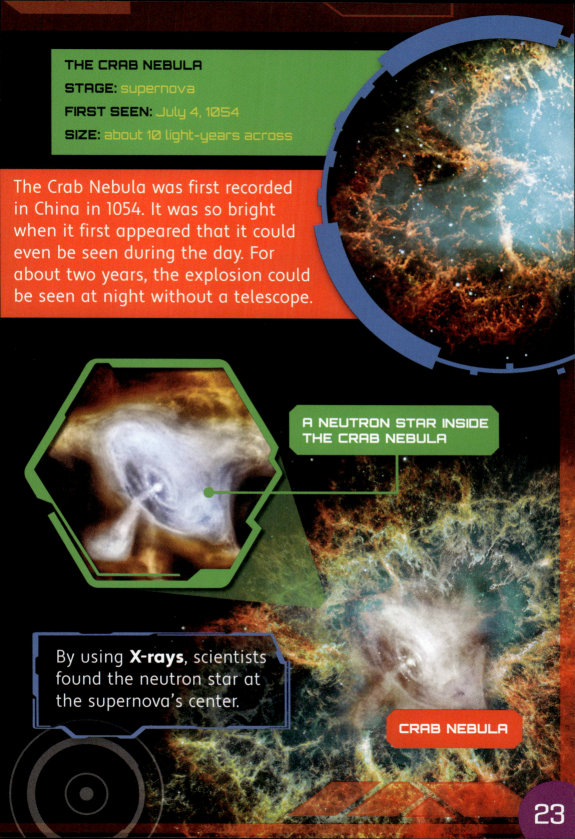

THE CRAB NEBULA
STAGE: supernova
FIRST SEEN: July 4, 1054
SIZE: about 10 light-years across

The Crab Nebula was first recorded in China in 1054. It was so bright when it first appeared that it could even be seen during the day. For about two years, the explosion could be seen at night without a telescope.

A NEUTRON STAR INSIDE THE CRAB NEBULA

By using **X-rays**, scientists found the neutron star at the supernova's center.

CRAB NEBULA

LUCY THE DIAMOND STAR

BPM 37093, ALSO KNOWN AS LUCY
TYPE: white dwarf
SIZE: about 2,500 miles (4,000 km) across
TEMPERATURE: less than 12,000°F (6,600°C)

MOON

Even the largest diamonds that have been found on Earth are small enough to fit in a human hand. The diamond star Lucy, however, is bigger than the moon!

SOME OF EARTH'S LARGEST DIAMONDS

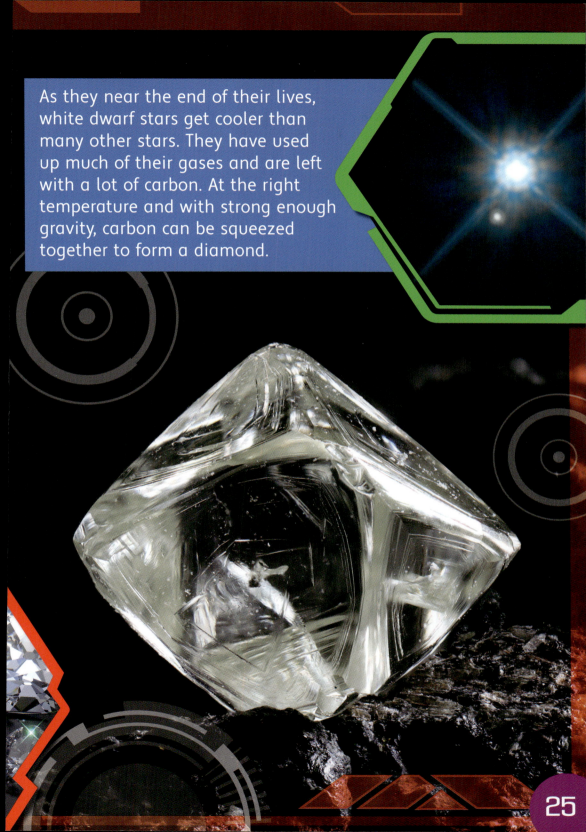

As they near the end of their lives, white dwarf stars get cooler than many other stars. They have used up much of their gases and are left with a lot of carbon. At the right temperature and with strong enough gravity, carbon can be squeezed together to form a diamond.

SECRET STAR SOUNDS

A.I. EILEEN:
Many people believe space is almost completely silent, and they are partly right. However, stars do make sounds. People just can't hear them in space!

On Earth, sound travels in waves moving through air. But in space there is no air for the waves to move through. Instead, stars trap sound inside themselves. Bigger stars make deeper noises while smaller stars hit higher notes.

Sounds bounce around inside a star's gases.

Astronomers can use information about the brightness of a star to guess what it sounds like. When gas bursts out of a star, it causes some areas to be lighter and some to be darker. Astronomers translate these changes in brightness into sound.

Watching the changing brightness can also tell scientists about a star's size, age, and gases. Scientists use brightness levels to tell if a star has any planets near it, too.

DYSON SWARMS

TABBY'S STAR

Astronomers have noticed big changes in the brightness of one star that is about 1,470 light-years from Earth. Tabby's Star suddenly began dimming very quickly. Some people wondered if its light was blocked by alien equipment called a Dyson Swarm.

Some scientists think very smart aliens could build a net of solar panels—a Dyson Swarm—that would wrap around a star and collect its energy.

If aliens existed, could they be using a Dyson Swarm around Tabby's Star?

A.I. EILEEN:
Our agents haven't found life on any planet except Earth. But that doesn't mean they aren't looking. . . .

28

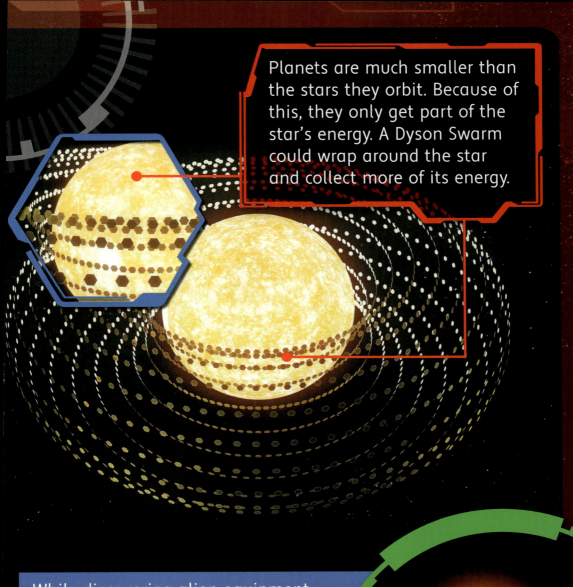

Planets are much smaller than the stars they orbit. Because of this, they only get part of the star's energy. A Dyson Swarm could wrap around the star and collect more of its energy.

While discovering alien equipment would be exciting, our findings show another reason the light from Tabby's Star is dimming. The light is probably passing through a dust cloud on its way to Earth.

DUST IN FRONT OF TABBY'S STAR

29

YOUR MISSION

Now that you're up to date with our star files, it's time to start your own. Some secret agents choose to find out more about how the sun affects Earth. Others learn about the death of stars. Agents even work in teams to build equipment for exploring space.

A team working on the James Webb Space Telescope

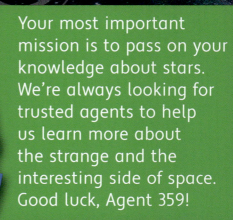

Your most important mission is to pass on your knowledge about stars. We're always looking for trusted agents to help us learn more about the strange and the interesting side of space. Good luck, Agent 359!

GLOSSARY

access the permission to go somewhere or use something

astronomers scientists who study outer space

cores the inside, central parts of planets and stars

equipment specific tools that can be used for certain jobs

fuel a material that can be used to power something

gravity the force that pulls smaller objects toward the center of larger objects

helium a light, colorless gas

hemisphere one of the two halves Earth is divided into

hydrogen a light, colorless, odorless gas

myths old stories that tell of strange or magical events and creatures

orbit to travel in a circle around an object in space

spiral shaped in a twisting circle

telescope a tool for looking closely at things that are very far away

universe the planets, moons, stars, and everything else in space

X-rays waves of strong energy that cannot be seen with just the eyes

INDEX

brightness 4, 9, 14–15, 17, 22–23, 27–28
color 7
constellations 14–16
death 22, 30
diamonds 24–25
Earth 6–7, 10, 12, 17, 19, 24, 26, 28–30
energy 22, 28–29
galaxies 18–19
gases 5, 7–9, 18, 21–22, 25–27
gravity 7–8, 18, 20, 25
solar system 10, 13
sun 10–13, 30
supergiants 9

READ MORE

Barr, Catherine. *Voyage Among the Stars (Space Voyage).* New York: Rosen Publishing, 2022.

Finan, Catherine C. *Stars and Galaxies (X-treme Facts: Space).* Minneapolis: Bearport Publishing, 2022.

Hudd, Emily. *How Long Do Stars Last? (How Long Does It Take?).* North Mankato, MN: Capstone Press, 2020.

LEARN MORE ONLINE

1. Go to **www.factsurfer.com** or scan the QR code below.
2. Enter **"Stars Space Files"** into the search box.
3. Click on the cover of this book to see a list of websites.